This Notebook Belongs To:

____

Made in the USA
Middletown, DE
24 August 2024

59653513R00071